Contents

KT-468-867

General editor: Graham Handley MA Ph.D.

Brodie's Notes on Ben Jonson's
Volpone

Ray Wilkinson

© Ray Wilkinson 1978

First published 1978 by
PAN BOOKS LTD

This revised edition published 1993 by
THE MACMILLAN PRESS LTD

Palgrave Macmillan in the UK is an imprint of Macmillan Publishers Limited, registered in England, company number 785998, of Houndmills, Basingstoke, Hampshire RG21 6XS.

Palgrave Macmillan in the US is a division of St Martin's Press LLC, 175 Fifth Avenue, New York, NY 10010.

Palgrave Macmillan is the global academic imprint of the above companies and has companies and representatives throughout the world.

Palgrave® and Macmillan® are registered trademarks in the United States, the United Kingdom, Europe and other countries.

ISBN-13   978–0-333-58131-5

This book is printed on paper suitable for recycling and made from fully managed and sustained forest sources. Logging, pulping and manufacturing processes are expected to conform to the environmental regulations of the country of origin.

A catalogue record for this book is available from the British Library.

Printed and bound in Great Britain by
CPI Antony Rowe, Chippenham and Eastbourne

Preface

The intention throughout this study aid is to stimulate and guide, to encourage your involvement in the book, and to develop informed responses and a sure understanding of the main details.

Brodie's Notes provide a clear outline of the play or novel's plot, followed by act, scene, or chapter summaries and/or commentaries. These are designed to emphasize the most important literary and factual details. Poems, stories or non-fiction texts combine brief summary with critical commentary on individual aspects or common features of the genre being examined. Textual notes define what is difficult or obscure and emphasize literary qualities. Revision questions are set at appropriate points to test your ability to appreciate the prescribed book and to write accurately and relevantly about it.

In addition, each of these Notes includes a critical appreciation of the author's art. This covers such major elements as characterization, style, structure, setting and themes. Poems are examined technically – rhyme, rhythm, for instance. In fact, any important aspect of the prescribed work will be evaluated. The aim is to send you back to the text you are studying.

Each study aid concludes with a series of general questions which require a detailed knowledge of the book: some of these questions may invite comparison with other books, some will be suitable for coursework exercises, and some could be adapted to work you are doing on another book or books. Each study aid has been adapted to meet the needs of the current examination requirements. They provide a basic, individual and imaginative response to the work being studied, and it is hoped that they will stimulate you to acquire disciplined reading habits and critical fluency.

Graham Handley 1990

A close reading of the set book is the student's primary task. These Notes will help to increase your understanding and appreciation of the play, and to stimulate *your own* thinking about it: *they are in no way intended as a substitute* for a thorough knowledge of the play.

If you can manage to see a production of the play, this would be very useful to you.

These notes are based on the Ernest Benn New Mermaids paperback edition of *Volpone*, but as references are given to individual Acts, scenes and lines, these Notes may be used with any edition of the play.

The author and his work

Jonson was born in London in 1572; his father died before he was born, and his mother soon afterwards married a bricklayer.

He was educated for a time at Westminster School, but did not go up to Oxford or Cambridge – probably because he was too poor. In 1589 he became apprenticed to a bricklayer, but very little more is known of his early life. He served with the army in Flanders. He became an actor, playing in Kyd's *Spanish Tragedy*, and he began to write. In 1598 he was described by Francis Meres as being among 'our best for tragedy', though his earliest works have disappeared. Also in 1598 he wrote *Every Man in His Humour*, his first great success, in which Shakespeare acted. And in that same year he killed his opponent in a duel: he was branded on the thumb and his goods were confiscated; he was lucky to avoid hanging.

Jonson was several times in trouble with the law; he had earlier been imprisoned for writing 'slanderous matter', and in the reign of James I he was imprisoned for satirizing the Scots in *Eastward Ho!* He carried on a running battle with his fellow playwrights Marston and Dekker, whose charges against him he refutes in the Prologue to *Volpone* (1605). Apart from *Volpone*, his most famous comedies were *The Alchemist* (1610), *Bartholomew Fair* (1614) and *The Devil Is An Ass* (1616). He had become a Catholic during his spell in prison in 1598 but he reverted to Protestantism about a dozen years later. In 1612 he took the unusual step for a playwright of preparing his *Collected Works* for publication. In the last years of his life he wrote many masques but his plays were mostly unsuccessful. He died in 1637 and was buried in Westminster Abbey.

Jonson was a learned man and a voracious reader. A full edition of *Volpone* will, very properly, give the sources of his many borrowings, from Lucian's *The Dreame*, the *Satires* of Juvenal, from Horace, Catullus, Erasmus's *In Praise of Folly*, from Pliny's *Natural History*, and so on. But it is doubtful whether the reader who knows nothing of these borrowings is missing anything of importance to the understanding or enjoyment of the play. To read the play we do not need to be able to read Latin; we need to be responsive to Jonson's racy and idiomatic English.

Setting and plot

Setting

The play is set in Venice and makes use of the institutions and topography of that great Renaissance city. Venice was famous as the centre of mercantile prosperity as well as for its art and architecture. The city also had a reputation for Machiavellian evil-doing; its exotic setting is appropriate and lends richness to this tale of deception, greed, lust and luxury, though the essentials of the play can be found in all places and at all times. It can also be convenient to use the institutions of a distant city: for instance, in the 'trial' scenes of Acts 4 and 5 there is no need to be faithful to actual, and tedious, legal procedures.

Plot

The play moves on the fizzing momentum of its plot – a momentum which is generated almost entirely through the energy of Volpone and the virtuosity of Mosca and which provides a bewildering variety of action. The plot is almost impossible to summarize, though an attempt has been made in the comments on individual scenes. A wholly adequate account of the plot would be as long as the play itself, since Jonson has a genius for farcical detail, for little grace-notes of incident or remark thrown off in the heat of the moment. He is like an expert conjuror who has little miracles of prestidigitation, to which he doesn't bother to draw attention, inside his bigger tricks. The joy of the play is in its thickness of texture. Something is always happening; sometimes several things at once. The plot is packed with details, but the details are kept in their place. They are not allowed to interfere with the total design, the mounting speed, the dizzy complication, the breath-taking escapes, the final crash.

The plot – which is the interplay of event and character – has reached the satisfying conclusion to which all its intricate twists and turns have been leading. We are not inclined to weep over Volpone as he is led off to prison, nor to spit after him; rather, we applaud him when he returns to speak the

Epilogue, because he is the one who has given us the entertainment. The play is in some ways like a game of chess, with strict and arbitrary rules. Volpone has been check-mated after a complicated series of moves. The game is therefore over.

It may be argued that there are two elements in the play that are excrescences; the sub-plot involving Sir Pol and Lady Would-be, and the interludes involving Nano, Castrone and Androgyno. It could be said the play would be better without the latter monstrosities: physical grotesqueness is unpleasant and unfunny, and the only scene of any length in which they appear (1, 2) is so formidably obscure and comes so early in the play that many readers may have given up attempting to read any further.

Scene summaries, critical commentary, textual notes and revision questions

The Argument

This is in the form of a clever little acrostic, in which the initial letters of the lines make the name 'Volpone'. The acrostic gives a brief résumé of the plot.

state Estate.

The Prologue

Lines 9–33

whose throats their envy failing Their envy gives them sore throats.

all ... railing Some critics and other playwrights had accused Jonson of writing plays which were merely 'railing', i.e. abuse.

He was a year about them Jonson had been accused of writing slowly by playwrights who prided themselves on their ability to knock off a play at great speed. Jonson, they said, produced plays only once a year, like a skin disease. He did, indeed, write comparatively slowly, since he believed in constant revision.

two months since, no feature Two months ago, the play did not exist.

And, though he dares give them five lives to mend it His critics would take five lifetimes to improve his play.

From his own hand ... coadjutor He used no collaborator unlike many of his contemporaries.

no eggs are broken ... affrighted There is no crude slapstick in the play.

gull Dupe.

ends Tags.

Bet'lem Bedlam, the madhouse. The 'forced' action might win the approval of mad people.

fable Plot.

quick Alive.

gall, and copperas Common ingredients of ink. Bad humour was attributed to the gall-bladder. Copperas was iron sulphate, a bitter substance. Jonson will remove these ingredients and replace them with salt ('wit') which is good for the complexion.

Act 1, Scene 1

Volpone is presumably in bed and is wakened by Mosca. He

greets the day and pays his morning worship to his store of gold. The blasphemy is conscious and deliberate, characteristically daring and outrageous. His hoard of gold is the shrine at which he worships. Gold is God, 'the world's soul, and mine'; the Spring, banishing Winter, is the light that banished darkness on the first day of creation, It is brighter than the Sun, the centre of the Universe. The joy to be taken in it is greater than the joy of any human relationship, 'or any other waking dream on earth'. The love of gold is the driving force in all men; it can buy the very soul, turn hell into heaven. The man who has gold has 'virtue, fame, honour, and all things else'.

The speech, like the speaker, is full-blooded, hyperbolic, full of relish; and it strikes the keynote of the play, in which we see how men sell themselves, and their wives and sons, for gold. It is a perversion of all real values, but in the world of the play it is almost completely true. In the end Volpone is overthrown, not by a higher system of values but by his own overweening delight in manipulation; because he has money he is not, until the very last, suspected of evil.

All Volpone's extravagance and gusto is directed towards evil ends, but the gusto is infectiously attractive. He is, moreover, no miser:

> I glory
> More in the cunning purchase of my wealth,
> Than in the glad possession: (30–32)

The words 'glory' and 'glad', with their weight of emphasis, are important: at least Volpone enjoys himself and the gold which he sets his wits to gain. The pleasure is the pleasure of the chase. He delights in, and boasts of, the fact that he makes money 'no common way'. He doesn't work – by trading, farming or running a factory. Mosca is able to claim on his behalf that he doesn't exploit the workers or grind down the poor. This is true, but not, as Mosca well knows, because Volpone is touched by pity but because he has developed a way of making money that is easier and much more fun.

Mosca flatters Volpone by calling him one who 'know(s) the use of riches'. His flattery is a means of extracting a tip from his master. Already the parasite ('an animal . . . living in or on another and drawing nutriment directly from it' – OED) is at work.

Volpone is ready to 'cocker up my genius'. He is rich; he has no heir. 'This draws new clients', with gifts,

> With hope, that when I die (which they expect
> Each greedy minute) it shall then return,
> Tenfold, upon them. (79–81)

'Greedy' is another keyword, since greed is the master passion of the play. What Volpone enjoys is 'playing with their hopes' – and, again, the word 'playing' is important: it is all a game to Volpone, and he is always, with brilliant virtuosity, play-acting. With what delight he lets 'the cherry knock against their lips' and watches them slobber!

Lines 1–88

Good morning It is sunrise. The action of the play takes place in a single day, in conformity with the Unity of Time.

shrine In speaking of his gold, Volpone uses the language of religion. The gold is like a sacred relic, to be worshipped.

Hail the world's soul, and mine There is a pun on 'sol' – the sun. Volpone regards gold as the controlling principle of the world, and of himself.

the celestial Ram Aries, a sign of the Zodiac through which the sun passes in the Spring.

thou sun of Sol Gold was held to be the son of the Sun.

purchase Procuring (by theft).

shambles Slaughterhouses.

to grind 'em into poulder To grind employees into powder by exploiting them.

subtle glass Delicate glass, for which Venice was famous.

melting Made soft by luxurious living.

your Dutch/Will pills of Butter The Dutch were renowned for their liking for butter.

Candian wines Candy is in Crete, and produced Malmsey.

observer A fawning follower.

cocker up my _genius_ Indulge my bent.

And counter-work, the one, unto the other They plot against each other in the hope of being made sole heir.

bearing them in hand Encouraging them.

Act 1, Scene 2

The opening passage of the scene is difficult for a modern audience, or student, to come to terms with. Rightly or wrongly, it is sometimes cut from modern productions. The first sixty-two lines are an 'entertainment' that Mosca has produced for his master. The lines are of doubtful relevance to the play as a whole, and very obscure.

The dwarf, the eunuch and the hermaphrodite are monsters – extreme forms of the monstrousness which runs throughout the play, since many of the other characters are beasts-cum-men. They are probably Volpone's bastard children, the perverted fruits of his haphazard virility. They speak crude doggerel couplets. Nano describes how the soul of Pythagoras (who believed in the transmigration of souls) descended through the bodies of various men and women of increasing meanness before inhabiting the body of Androgyno, the grotesque hermaphrodite. The last incarnations are as an ass and as a Puritan – a type Jonson detested. This reduction of all things to folly and monstrosity may be said to fit the scheme of the play as a whole, but can hardly be said to be integrated with the rest of the play at all clearly.

Voltore arrives, the first of the morning visitors to Volpone's levee. He has brought a huge piece of plate. Volpone makes the first of several references in the play to the fable of the fox, 'stretched on the earth', who flattered the crow so that it opened its mouth to sing and dropped its piece of cheese. Mosca helps to dress Volpone in the furs appropriate to a fox and acts as make-up man, using ointment to make Volpone's eyes look rheumy. While he flits busily about his private theatre, Mosca delightedly mocks Voltore's hopes of inheriting Volpone's wealth – the wealth that can achieve everything, can even make an ass seem learned.

Then Volpone goes into his act, subsiding into the grunts and groans of the extraordinary mixture of diseases he pretends to have. He is a skilled actor, and loves playing a part. There is a comic contrast between his real vitality and the decrepitude he assumes. No doubt he overacts, since it is his nature to overdo everything.

Lines 4–34

false pace The verse is deliberately loose and awkward.

Pythagoras (540–510 BC). He put forward the doctrine of the transmigration of the soul.

fast and loose Hard to catch; from a game in which the victim had to spear a belt, but the 'juggler' could always deceive him.

Aethalides Pythagoras claimed to remember having entered the bodies of others. Aethalides was the son of Mercury, herald to the Argonauts and believed to be able to remember everything.

Euphorbus Warrior in the Trojan War, referred to in *The Iliad*.

the cuckold of Sparta This refers to Menelaus, whose wife Helen was taken to Troy by Paris, thereby precipitating the Trojan War.

Hermotimus A Geek philosopher.

charta Paper.

Pyrrhus, of Delos A philosopher.

the Sophist of Greece Pythagoras.

Hight Called.

Aspasia Mistress of Pericles.

Was, again, of a whore ... philosopher From a whore she became a philosopher again.

itself Probably refers to the cock who is the narrator in the *Dream*, by Lucian (*c.* AD 117–80). The cock tells the story to a cobbler (see line 24).

Quater Pythagoras's triangular symbol of harmony.

his golden thigh Pythagoras was said by his followers to have a golden thigh.

reformation The Protestant reformation.

forbid meats Pythagoras forbade his disciples to eat fish, flesh and beans.

On fish ... Carthusian The Carthusians were a strict sect, but they were allowed to eat fish.

Lines 35–130

Why, then thy dogmatical silence hath left thee Pythagoras ordered his disciples to be silent for five years.

moyle Mule.

precise Puritanical.

nativity-pie Christmas pie.

Fools ... He, he, he It is not clear who sings the song: perhaps Mosca himself.

Selves, and others merry making Making themselves, and others, happy.

bable The Fool's bauble; also the phallus. Fools are supposed to make up for their lack of brains by their sexual potency.

free from slaughter Without being punished for it.

changing Being changed.

gor-crow Eating gore: i.e. a carrion crow.

A piece of plate, sir Voltore has brought a piece of plate, as an offering.

Good! and not a fox ... gaping crow A reference to the fable of the crow that dropped its piece of cheese when it sang because of the fox's flattery. Volpone implies that such an engraving would be more appropriate.

fetch Persuade Volpone to make Voltore his heir.

foot-cloths Drapery for a horse, signifying wealth.

have clear way ... as himself Have the way cleared even for his mule, which is as educated as he is.

reverend purple The robes of a Doctor of Divinity.
ointment for your eyes The ointment makes his eyes look sick.
phthisic Asthma.
posture Imposture.
uh! O— Coughs and groans.

Act 1, Scene 3

For Voltore's benefit Volpone hams the part of the dying man who can manage little more than pathetically weak interjections. He pretends that the only sense he has left is the sense of touch, so that Voltore puts the plate into his hand. Voltore is convinced that Volpone's possessions are now almost his.

Mosca speaks a speech in praise of the lawyer's profession: he admires the way the lawyer can turn everything to gold, prove black to be white without breaking the law, and accept bribes from both sides. The speech is characteristic of both Volpone and Mosca: they deceive, but they are not themselves deceived. It is a sarcastic parody of the lawyer's trade, but Mosca knows that Voltore, who is utterly corrupt, will take it as a genuine compliment. And the compliment *is*, in a sense, sincere, since Volpone and Mosca practise the same trade of deception – but they do it more successfully and on a larger scale, so that they reap the benefits of the lawyer's very skill. If Mosca is a parasite, Voltore is a sub-parasite.

Lines 4–66
notes Signs.
grateful Welcome.
St Mark There were many goldsmiths in St Mark's square.
Hath taste Can be seen – or has good taste.
your keys They are Voltore's because they are Volpone's; everything of Volpone's will soon be Voltore's.
course Probably means 'profession' here.
put it up Pocket it.
perplexed Involved.
chequeen A Venetian gold coin.

Act 1, Scene 4

Corbaccio, the next visitor, is a ridiculous figure, aged, tottery, deaf. He is genuinely on his last legs, yet he thinks himself 'lusty' and hopes, ludicrously, to outlive Volpone and inherit his wealth. He understands, however, the urgent necessity that Volpone should die soon, for he has brought drugs to help him on his way. Mosca takes the opportunity to add a parody of doctors to his parody of lawyers:

> they flay a man
> Before they kill him. (27–8)

Nearly everybody in the play is either a fool or a knave.

Corbaccio dances from leg to leg with glee at Mosca's account of Volpone's physical degeneration. When he hears of Voltore's plate he tries to outbid him with a bag of chequeens. Mosca says that the gold will be the elixir to recover Volpone, at which Corbaccio tries to take his gift back. Mosca prevents this and persuades him that the best way to win Volpone's favour is to leave him all his money. Volpone, he says, will be much impressed by Corbaccio's willingness to disinherit 'A son so brave, and highly meriting'. Corbaccio claims to have already thought of this generous scheme: he will really be doing his son a favour by 'investing' his money in this way. Like others in the play he has an infinite capacity for self-deception. Mosca, relying on Corbaccio's deafness, is able to abuse him openly.

Volpone, meanwhile, has scarcely been able to contain himself while pretending to be asleep. His suppressed energy bursts out as he leaps out of bed, lost in admiration of Mosca's skill. 'What a rare punishment,' he reflects, 'is avarice!', and he reflects elegiacally on the deceptions and miseries of age, though in his pride and self-confidence he doesn't apply his reflections to himself.

Corvino is at the door, so Volpone leaps back into bed, after having his make-up renewed by the ever solicitous Mosca.

Lines 7–162
What? mends he Corbaccio is deaf.
opiate This is designed, of course, to finish Volpone off.
brook Put up with.
flay Strip the skin off – i.e. rob him of his money.
resolved Loose, rooting.
scotomy Dizziness.
left Ceased.
By your own scale, sir Judging by yourself.
elixir In alchemy, the substance which was supposed to make

life eternal. Presumably, since Corbaccio does not want Volpone to live, the remark is an aside.

'Tis aurum palpabile, if not potabile The gold can be touched if not drunk (as a medicine).

colour Appearance.

taking Attractive.

O, but colour Corbaccio wants to be reassured that it is only an appearance.

enforce Emphasise.

your proper issue Your genuine son.

his His heir.

he Mosca.

Still, my invention Still my own idea.

Rook go with you May you be deceived.

I know ... sir The reference is to Jacob's cheating of Esau.

Let out my sides Perhaps Volpone is so trussed up that he cannot laugh freely.

flux Flow.

covers any hook Disguises the nature of the hook.

give 'em words Deceive them with words.

going Ability to walk.

Aeson His youth was renewed by Medea's magic.

battens Grows fat.

turns air Turns to delusion.

bout Application of ointment.

Act 1, Scene 5

Volpone is now pretending to be so near death that Corvino wonders whether it is really worth while parting with his pearl and diamond, but Mosca persuades him. Mosca describes how Corvino has been made Volpone's heir. Urged on by Mosca, Corvino shouts abuse in Volpone's ear; between them they give a horrific picture of illness and decrepitude, adding to the picture of decay which permeates the play. Apart from greed, Corvino's besetting vice is jealousy of his lovely wife: at the mere mention of her name he disappears to find out what she is up to.

Lady Would-be is at the door, but we are spared her 'everlasting voice' for the time being. Volpone marvels that the English should be so ready to 'let loose/Their wives to all encounters!' (lines 101–2), but Mosca points out that 'She hath not yet the face, to be dishonest'.

This brings mention of the beauty, by contrast, of Corvino's wife, Celia. Mosca describes her beauty in richly sensuous verse, in a passage which rivals the exultation of the first speech of the play, in praise of gold. Celia is described as having 'flesh that melteth, in the touch, to blood' (line 113): she is 'Bright as your gold! and lovely as your gold!' (114). Sexual desire is the only force that can rival avarice in the play, and conflict between the two is one of the things that undo Volpone.

We learn that Corvino guards Celia as closely as Volpone guards his gold. There are even guards to guard the guards. Volpone determines to see her – in disguise, of which he is a master.

Lines 9–125
orient From the East, whence come the best pearls.
visor Mask.
fable Story.
it hath deserved it Your incontinence has deserved syphilis.
culverin Gun.
bore it Pierce the wax of his ear.
draught Privy, cess-pool.
keep him Look after him.
this Mention of his wife has sent the jealous Corvino hurrying to see what she is up to.
fat Get fat
She hath not yet the face, to be dishonest She is not pretty enough to be unfaithful.
O'er the first year Young.
each of which is set ... examined Each servant is questioned about the other servants.

Revision questions on Act 1

1 What is there in Volpone's character, as displayed in the opening scene, that makes him more than a simple miser?
2 What does Act 1 show us of the relationship between Volpone and Mosca?
3 What function has the 'entertainment' of Act 1, scene 2? Discuss its relation, in tone and content, to the play as a whole.

Act 2, Scene 1

We meet Sir Politic Would-Be, with his aspirations to worldly wisdom, his credulity, his ability to see plots everywhere, his pomposity and affectation. Peregrine at first can hardly believe his ears, but soon decides to humour him with accounts of strange prodigies at home. Sir Pol believes the whale in the Thames was sent by Spinola, the Spanish commander in the Netherlands, as a plot against London. He thinks Stone, the fool, was a Dutch spy who received messages in cabbages and passed them on by cutting his meat in code. Sir Pol is a gullible know-all who regards Peregrine as an innocent beginner in the ways of the world.

Lines 1–51
salt Inordinate.
Laid for this height of Venice Setting course for the latitude of Venice.
quote Make notes.
licence The equivalent of a passport.
vents Comes out of.
seconded Confirmed.
raven A bird of ill omen.
gull Dupe.
speaks Describes.
tires Attires.
Another whelp According to Stow's *Annals* the lions in the Tower whelped twice at about the time the play was written, causing a considerable sensation.
The fires at Berwick In 1604 there was alarm when ghostly battles were seen near Berwick. The illusions were perhaps caused by the Northern Lights.
the new star Kepler discovered a new star in 1604.
porcpisces A porpoise had recently been taken from the Thames.
There was a whale discovered … Of the Stode fleet A whale, according to Peregrine, had waited at Woolwich to sink the fleet of the English Merchant Adventurers, who had settled at Stode, on the Elbe. (A whale had, in reality, been seen in the river above London Bridge.)
the Archdukes Isabella and Albert, who ruled the Spanish Netherlands.
Spinola's whale Spinola commanded the Spanish army in the Netherlands and was popularly credited with devices of extraordinary ingenuity.

Lines 53–121
Stone A celebrated Fool of the time.
apprehend Feel.
in cabbages Concealed in cabbages, which were imported from Holland.

pome-citrons Limes.
ordinary Tavern.
advertisement Instructions.
concealed statesman A disguised agent of the state.
Character Code.
In polity As a 'blind'.
Mamuluchi Slaves who came to rule Egypt. They have nothing
   to do with either baboons or China. Sir Politic's imagination is
   running away with him.
discovery Revelation.
advices News.
coat Side.
relations Reports.
Myself ... fortunes 'I am obliged to my good luck'.
that vulgar grammer A grammar of the vernacular.
cried Read aloud.
bark Outward appearance.
ingenuous Noble.
high kind Important capacity.

Act 2, Scene 2

Mosca enters to stage-manage Volpone's 'act' as a mountebank. He quickly erects a scaffold stage under Celia's window.
Sir Pol is excited at the prospect of seeing an Italian mountebank at work: he believes mountebanks to be 'the only know-
ing men of Europe', and treats Peregrine's scepticism with
lofty, contemptuous pity.

Volpone puts on his virtuoso performance as Scoto of
Mantua, selling his fake elixir. He proves a magnificent fast-
talking salesman. He is, one feels, as much an entertainer as a
deceiver, inebriated with the exuberance of his verbosity, and
much of his patter is extraordinarily modern, showing that the
breed has changed little over the centuries. 'I protest, I, and
my six servants, are not able to make of this precious liquor so
fast, as it is fetched away from my lodgings by gentlemen of
your city ... this is the physician, this the medicine ... both
together may be termed an abstract of the theoric and practic
of the Aesculapian art ... I never valued this ampulla, or vial,
at less than eight crowns, but for this time I am content to be
deprived of it for six; six crowns is the price; and less, in
courtesy, I know you cannot offer me ... you shall not give me
six crowns, nor five, nor four, nor three, nor two, nor one; nor
half a ducat, six – pence it will cost you ...'

Sir Pol is entranced, but Celia, from her window, is the first to throw her handkerchief. Volpone is interrupted by the jealous Corvino in his encomium on the virtues of his powder 'that made Venus a goddess ... kept her perpetually young ... cleared her wrinkles, firmed her gums, filled her skin, coloured her hair ... (that) seats your teeth, did they dance like virginal jacks, firm as a wall ...'

It may be asked, however, what all this has to do with the play as a whole: it seems an excessively elaborate way of introducing Volpone to Celia. Of course, it is another example of Volpone's brazenly deceiving the gullible with false promises, and his elixir is as delusive a panacea as his gold. His incarnation as a mountebank is particularly appropriate. But in any case the scene can be allowed to stand by itself as an entertaining tour-de-force.

Lines 2–77

bank Bench.

quacksalvers People who quack about ointments – the origin of 'quack'.

venting Vending, selling.

lewd Ignorant.

terms, and shreds Scraps of jargon.

beliers They lie about the favours they have received from great men as much as about their vile medicines.

utter Sell.

Scoto of Mantua The name of a famous Italian juggler who visited England in 1576.

zany Clown.

the Portico to the Procuratia The arcaded doorway of the Procurators of St Mark's.

cold on my feet Having cold feet, and therefore anxious to sell cheaply.

Buttone An imaginary rival.

a sforzato By force.

Cardinal Bembo's – cook Cardinal Bembo was a Venetian humanist. The dash suggests that Volpone was going to say 'mistress'.

attached Constrained.

ground *ciarlitani* Charlatans who work upon the ground, without a bench.

Tabarine, the fabulist Tabarine was a clown contemporary with Scoto. He told stories.

several *scartoccios* Separate papers.

earthly oppilations Mundane matters.

canaglia The vulgar mob.

Terra Firma The mainland, as opposed to Venice itself.

Lines 81–130

magazines Cellars.

moscadelli Muscatel wines.

cocted Boiled.

unguento ointment.

malignant humours All diseases were supposed to be caused by one of the four humours, which corresponded to the four elements. The four humours were blood, choler, phlegm and melancholy.

fricace Massage.

vertigine Dizziness.

mal caduco Epilepsy.

retired nerves Shrunk muscles.

strangury Impeded urination.

iliaca passio Colic.

tortion Twisting.

receipt Recipe.

Aesculapian Aesculapius was the god of medicine.

Zan Fritada Volpone calls Mosca by the name of a famous Italian clown.

Broughton A contemporary scholar whose works were a by-word for unintelligibility.

Hippocrates ... Galen Greek medical writers.

Tobacco, sassafras Tobacco, and sassafras (from the roots of a small North American tree of that name), had both been recently imported from America, and were thought to have medicinal virtues.

guacum A drug extracted from the resin of the tropical American quaiacum tree. This was used to treat rheumatism and diarrhoea.

Raymond Lully An alchemist of the thirteenth century who was supposed to have discovered the elixir of life.

Gonswart Nobody knows who he was. Perhaps he was invented for the rhyme.

Paracelsus A celebrated sixteenth-century Swiss physician.

the signiory of the *Sanita* The health authorities of Venice.

divers Several people.

several simples Separate remedies.

balloo A game.

withall Also.

gossip Intimate acquaintance.

offices Duties.

gazets Pennies.

coil Fuss.

Tart Sharp.

Moist of hand The sign of youth and ardour.

Here's a medicine, for the nones The medicine will prevent you from getting venereal disease.

moccenigo A coin worth about ninepence.

banner/of my front Either his doctor's hat or his advertisement for his medicines.
bagatine Very small coin.
handkerchiefs Containing money.
pistolet A gold coin.
poulder Powder.
moiety Part.
sophisticated Adulterated.
virginal jacks The keys of the virginals.

Act 2, Scene 3

Corvino sees the whole business as a scene from the *Commedia dell'Arte*. Volpone is the lover, his wife the maid who is no better than she should be, and himself 'the lean and slippered pantaloon' whose part it is to be laughed at throughout the town as the cuckold.

There seems no reason why Sir Pol should see all this as 'some trick of state', but he doesn't need a reason, any more than Corvino needs a reason to be jealous. He sees stratagems all round him and believes that

> This three weeks, all my advices, all my letters,
> They have been intercepted. (13–14)

You can't be too careful when you're an Englishman abroad in wicked Italy!

Lines 1–8
Spite o' the devil Refers to Celia, the rest to Volpone.
Signior Flaminio A leading figure in Italian popular comedy. Corvino sees the situation as a play.
Franciscina The maid in popular comedy.
Pantalone di Besogniosi The 'lean and slippered pantaloon', who was often cuckolded.

Act 2, Scene 4

Volpone does nothing by halves, and he has fallen in love – or lust – desperately. He has momentarily, and dangerously, lost control of himself. With a superb image of sexual frustration and desire he describes how inside him, Cupid

> flings about his burning heat,
> As in a furnace, an ambitious fire
> Whose vent is stopped. (5–7)

One vice drives out another, and Volpone promises Mosca all his possessions if he will 'but crown my longings'. Mosca undertakes to achieve this. The task is apparently impossible, in view of Corvino's obsessive jealousy but it is the kind of challenge to his ingenuity that Mosca relishes.

Lines 3–34
bolting Darting arrows.
ambitious fire A rising fire, searching for an outlet.
liver The seat of the passions.
My better Angel Hope.
crown Perfect. There is a pun on 'coin'.
horn him Make him cuckold.
Is not the colour ... known Volpone's colour is red – the fox's colour.
mine My plot.
happiness Success.
epilogue Beating.

Act 2, Scene 5

Corvino's paranoid, self-lacerating jealousy is in full spate. The intensity of feeling is extraordinary – his fantasy is ridiculous yet hideous. He is jealous, not only of the 'juggling, tooth-drawing, prating mountebank' but of the crowd, 'noted lechers' who, he imagines, 'stood leering up'. As vicious imagination possesses him he is hardly conscious of what he is saying; the self-generating quality of his jealousy is revealed. Indecent puns are spewed about, together with abuse and murderous threats.

Celia's sweet reasonableness has no effect, since her husband's jealousy has no basis in reason. He is soon imagining the handkerchief being returned, with a letter appointing a place of meeting. When Celia gently points out that she is unlikely to meet anyone since she is scarcely allowed to leave the house, Corvino proposed a wildly grotesque scheme: to board the windows up; chalk a line beyond which Celia may not pass; make her wear a chastity belt; and insist that she do everything backwards. And if she so much as dares to look towards the window he will tear her to pieces and read a lecture about her iniquities 'to the city, and in public', thereby wilfully publicizing himself as a cuckold – the very thing he is so desperate to avoid. Jealousy, like greed, is a consuming and self-destructive monster.

Lines 2–71

tooth-drawing Mountebanks also drew teeth.

With his strained action, and his dole of faces With his extravagant gestures and repertoire of expressions.

satyrs Lustful men.

their call, their whistle Alluding to the song of the decoy bird which lures the game-bird down.

saffron Orange-coloured, golden.

toad-stone The stone that was thought to lie between a toad's eyes and to have medicinal properties.

cope-stitch A stitch used in embroidering a gown.

tilt-feather A plume worn in a tilting helmet. A feather worn in a hat was thought to be the sign of the fool.

starched beard Gummed beard, then in fashion.

The fricace for the mother Massage for hysteria, which was believed to have its origin in the womb. Sexual overtones are apparent throughout the passage.

mount Mount the bench, like a mountebank; but again a sexual pun.

cittern A guitar-like instrument, often carried by the mountebank's girl.

be a dealer Trade with; suggesting prostitution.

save your dowry An adulteress was deprived of her inheritance.

Dutchman The Dutch were supposed to be easy going and hard to move.

What couldst ... than What do you think I would do less than.

goatish Goats were renowned for their lust.

light Window. It acts as a bawd by revealing Celia to the world.

conjuror ... circle's safety The magician was thought to be safe in his circle until the devil had returned to hell.

lock A chastity belt.

backwards Celia must keep her back to the window – and do everything backwards.

passengers Passers-by.

an anatomy A subject for dissection.

lecture The lecture would be both anatomical and moral.

Act 2, Scene 6

Mosca enters. If he had witnessed the scene which has just taken place, even he might have thought that his task was hopeless. He announces Volpone's recovery and attributes it – it is a beautiful ironical touch – to Scoto's oil, which he says has been brought to Volpone by Corvino's rivals. Corvino's incredulity expresses itself in a derisively brisk recipe for the oil:

> Some few sod earwigs, pounded caterpillars,
> A little capon grease, and fasting spittle. (19–20)

Mosca alleges that, according to the best physicians in the land, the only thing that will recover Volpone is a young woman, 'Lusty and full of juice to sleep by him' – a remedy that is no more absurd and a good deal more attractive than some of the others that, he says, have been tried.

Mosca claims that he has come hot-foot, out of the kindness of his heart, to give Corvino first refusal; but Corvino had better be quick because they are 'all/Now striving, who shall first present him'. Mosca does nothing so crude as to suggest that Corvino should offer the services of his wife, but cunningly leads Corvino on to make the suggestion himself, inventing a Signior Lupo who has already offered his virgin daughter and saying that, in any case, Volpone can *do* nothing in bed since 'a long forgetfulness hath seized that part'. Under the influence of greed Corvino manages to 'command' his 'blood' and – an outrageous example of the pot and the kettle – abuses Signior Lupo as a 'covetous wretch'. He offers Celia, insisting that Volpone knows that the offer comes of 'Mine own free notion'. Mosca insists that Corvino doesn't come until he's sent for.

Notice that Mosca's long, beguiling 'temptation' speech (lines 25–47) is one long, winding, apparently artless sentence, innocently helpful, yet with every cadence perfectly calculated to shatter all Corvino's hopes of a fortune, and all his jealous scruples about his wife.

Lines 14–48
osteria Inn.
sod Boiled.
fasting spittle The spittle of the starving Scoto.
officious Dutiful.
cataplasm Poultice.
delate Report.
present him i.e. with some young woman.
conclude somewhat Think of something.

Lines 53–90
again On the other hand.
quean Whore.
his spirit i.e. his sexual potency. The doctor knows his virgin daughter is in no danger.
coming Coming round.
engaged The doctor has not yet gambled anything to secure Volpone's wealth.

motioned Proposed.
make your count Count on it.
wit Intelligence.

Act 2, Scene 7

Corvino is utterly changed, yet the same irrational monster. He coos at the weeping Celia 'I talked so but to try thee'. He says that he is not jealous, since jealousy is 'a poor unprofitable humour' – and profit is now the thing uppermost in his mind. In fact, his faith is not in Celia's constancy, but in the inconstancy of women who, if they 'have a will' (sexual appetite), 'They'll do 'gainst all the watches o' the world' (lines 8–9). The ironies are complex: in the previous scene he had said sarcastically that he would bring Scoto to cure her; now he is taking Celia to 'cure' Volpone/Scoto. And now that he is rid of his jealousy he is obviously very pleased with himself, though his present gentleness is surely even less attractive than his former madness.

Lines 4–8
lightness ... confirmed thee The triviality of the reason for my wrath should have reassured you.
will Sexual desire.

Revision questions for Act 2

1 Scene 1 introduces the sub-plot involving Politic-Would-Be and Peregrine. What echoes or parallels can you find between this scene and the concerns of Act 1? Try also to show how the material of the sub-plot *differs* from the action of the principal plot.

2 Does the scene where Volpone poses as a mountebank, or quack medicine seller, do more than allow the main character to demonstrate his skill at selling?

3 'Corvino is a satire on the absurdity both of extreme jealousy and greed.' Discuss, with reference to Act 2.

Act 3, Scene 1

Mosca is overjoyed with his success and has a scene to himself in which to celebrate his 'dear self'. He takes an artistic pride in his work – a pride that probably has a great deal in common with the playwright's delight in his own skill.

Mosca is 'limber', supple and endlessly flexible as he moves effortlessly from one part to another. He can 'change a visor swifter than a thought' and 'slip out of my skin, now, like a subtle snake'. He sees himself as a kind of Ariel of the parasite world, transcending the limitations of place, since he can 'be here/And there, and here, and yonder, all at once'. He sees the whole world as composed of 'parasites and subparasites', and he belongs to the highest class of the species, since he 'had the art born with him'. Lesser parasites merely 'echo my Lord', but Mosca is an independent spirit, all air and no earth.

'Success,' he says at the beginning of the speech, 'hath made me wanton': he might have taken warning from himself that he was in danger of over-reaching.

Lines 2–33
parts Abilities.
whimsy Whirling, elation.
limber Supple.
mystery Profession.
bare town-art The limited skills of the town parasite.
mould Invent.
bait that sense Tempt their ears.
Kitchen-invention Servants' food.
the groin The servants' stale food would include aphrodisiacs, perhaps.
fleer Leer.
legs and faces Bows and smirks.
zanies Clowns.

Act 3, Scene 2

Bonario appears and abuses Mosca who, immediately transforming himself, bursts into tears, pretending that Bonario is attacking him because he is poor. Bonario, being a man of 'simple innocence', can't tell the truth from the imitation and asks forgiveness. Mosca tells him that his father, Corbaccio, is about to disinherit him and persuades him to accompany him to Volpone's house to see, or at least hear, for himself.

Lines 14–67
unequal Unjust.
careful Won with care.

observance Service, parasitism.
mining Undermining.
Trained Led on.
Prove Undertake.
main Serious.
The work no way engageth me, but It isn't any of my business, but ....
for which mere respect For this reason only.
piety Filial piety.
professed Proclaimed.
front Forehead.

Act 3, Scene 3

Volpone is impatient for Mosca's return with news of his mission to Corvino. He calls for some sport from Nano, Androgyno and Castrone, to beguile the time. More doggerel follows, mercifully interrupted by a knock at the door. Volpone hopes that it is Mosca but, frustratingly, it is the ineffable Lady Would-be. Volpone takes to his bed, fearing the worst; his appetite for milking his clients has disappeared.

Lines 4–26
whether Which.
delicates Luxuries.
feat Nimble, dainty.
dwell Encamp.

Act 3, Scene 4

Volpone feigns illness again, but this time to escape the 'ever-lasting voice' of Lady Would-be. Nano describes her as 'the beauteous lady', but it is clear that her beauty is only a few layers of cosmetics deep. She makes an extraordinary fuss over a misplaced hair and lectures her serving-women, reminding them of how often she has 'preached these things'. She is one of those women who talk so much that nobody listens to a word they say. She is impervious to eroticism, to hints or even to direct rudeness. When Volpone says that, in the poet's view, 'your highest female grace is silence', she leaps in with 'Which o' your poets? Petrarch? or Tasso? or Dante?' She sails on regardless, pursuing her own erratic, unstoppable course. She has a grasshopper mind. She rarely finishes a sentence, but constantly strikes out in new directions according to some process of free association of her own. She is ready with an endless stream of old wives' remedies for Volpone's ills. She has noticed that the eyes of those to whom she talks 'three, four hours together' sometimes glaze over; but she is too insensitive, overwhelming and self centred to draw the obvious conclusion. It is difficult not to feel sorry for Volpone – even for Volpone – as he tries vainly to ride out the storm. He has met his match, and more than his match. 'Some power, some fate, some fortune rescue me,' he cries and, pat on cue, Mosca comes in.

Lines 2–55

band Collar.

favourably Pleasingly. The remark is presumably ironic.

tire Head-dress or coiffure.

bird-eyed Probably short-sighted.

fame Reputation.

curious Discriminating about details.

fucus A paste used for make-up.

golden mediocrity Aristotle's Golden Mean; though it is difficult to imagine what it has to do with Lady Would-be's dream.

the passion of the heart Heartburn.

Seed-pearl A small pearl that used to be used in medicine. There follows a list of things that were once used medicinally.

I have ta'en a grass-hopper by the wing A proverbial saying, meaning that it is better to leave nuisances alone.

Lines 74–125

concent Harmony.

The poet Sophocles (496–405 BC). A famous Athenian dramatist and tragic poet.

Pastor fido A pastoral play by Guarini.

trusted 'em, with much Entrusted them with a great deal; was much imitated.

Aretine Aretino wrote a number of indecent poems, which accompanied indecent pictures by Guilio Romano.

politic bodies States.

coaetanei Co-evals; of the same age.

Act 3, Scene 5

Volpone opens his heart to Mosca with his usual superb line in imaginative hyperbole:

> All my house
> But now, steamed, like a bath, with her thick breath.

Volpone is so desperate for freedom that he doesn't even care whether Lady Would-be has 'presented'. In fact, she has brought a cap, inevitably of her own making – a gift that can scarcely be compared with the offerings of the other legacy-hunters. Mosca is instantly ready with 'a quick fiction' (he never seems to have to stop to think) to get rid of her: he says that he has seen Sir Pol in a gondola with a whore, and Lady Would-be hurries off as quickly as Corvino in the earlier scene, though she makes a briefly threatening comeback.

Mosca has good news. Celia is coming. But first Corbaccio is expected with his rewritten will.

Lines 12–36
presented Presented her gift.
A toy A trifle.
take Succeed.
lightly Usually.
still Always.
primero A gambling game similar to poker. Some technical terms from the game follow.

Act 3, Scene 6

Bonario arrives and is hidden so that, in theory, he can overhear how his father has disinherited him.

Act 3, Scene 7

But it is Corvino, with Celia in tow, at the door. Although he was told to wait until he was sent for, he has come early to prostitute his wife lest the others should 'prevent' him. Mosca hurriedly persuades Bonario to step aside temporarily into a gallery. Corvino has explained to Celia why they have come and, in this topsy-turvy world, makes her compliance a strange test of her wifehood and obedience: he needs Celia to lie with Volpone so that he can protect his investments. He dismisses the idea of 'honour', in Falstaffian terms, as 'a breath ... a mere term/Invented to awe fools'. He can even persuade himself that what he is asking Celia to do is 'a pious work, mere charity'.

He thinks of Celia as a mere possession, like his gold or his clothes. Moreover, he tells Celia that Volpone is incapable of action; he:

> takes his meat
> With others' fingers; only knows to gape
> When you do scald his gums. (43–45)

The description of decrepitude is, characteristically, vigorously obscene.

In the end Corvino has to drag the reluctant Celia forcibly to Volpone's bed. He utters terrible threats which do not move Celia, since she would submit to any torture rather than give herself to Volpone. Corvino changes his tone; first to ludicrous self-pity, mixed with even more ludicrous self-righteousness:

> Be not thus obstinate, I ha' not deserved it:
> Think, who it is, entreats you. (108–9)

then to pathetic, cooing, monosyllabic entreaty:

> Do, but, go kiss him.
> Or touch him, but. For my sake. At my suit.
> This once. (111–13)

then back to abuse and threats. The extremes to which he is prepared to go to sell his wife – at whom, an hour before, he had been screaming with jealousy because she had leaned out of a window – are an extraordinary justification of Volpone's assertion, in the opening lines of the play, that gold 'mak'st men do all things'.

Celia is left alone with Volpone, who leaps from his bed, virile and eloquent, to woo her. He attributes his sudden health to 'thy beauty's miracle', and Celia has indeed wrought a miracle in him, since he now speaks contemptuously of one who would 'have sold his part of Paradise/For ready money'. He sees himself as Protean, jovial (in the sense of 'like Jove'); he pursues her about the room; he sings her a well-turned song (much of it translated from Catullus) on the theme ' 'Tis no sin, love's fruits to steal.' Celia's reluctance only inspires him to higher flights. He shows her the glories of his hoard of treasure:

> See here, a rope of pearl; and each, more orient
> Than that brave Egyptian queen caroused: (191–2)

The reference here is to Cleopatra's drinking a pearl of priceless value, dissolved in vinegar, when Antony had challenged her to spend a million sesterces at a single meal, and the associations are of extravagance and erotic luxury. There is no miserable miserliness about Volpone. His speech is sensuously beautiful: the diamond he shows her is such as:

> would have bought Lollia Paulina
> When she came in, like star-light, hid with jewels, (195–6)

The erotic associations of rich food are also employed, with Volpone's customary hyperbole:

> and, could we get the phoenix,
> Though nature lost her kind, whe were our dish. (204–5)

Celia mentions 'conscience', which Volpone, hardly interrupting the stride of his verse, dismisses as 'the beggar's virtue'. He describes the incredible richness of her baths, filled with the 'juice of July-flowers', with 'milk of unicorns' (somewhat difficult to obtain!) and

> panthers' breath
> Gathered in bags and mixed with Cretan wines. (215–16)

He goes on to describe the many disguises – he loves transforming himself – in which they will make love.

All this is, from the moral point of view, reprehensible; but we are swept along by the force of Volpone's imagination into sympathy with him. We may well find lust a more attractive vice than avarice, though we shouldn't forget that in Volpone's case it leads, when thwarted, to attempted rape. Volpone's vice is an excess of life, not, as in the case of Corvino Corbaccio and Voltore, a deathly meanness of spirit. Even the hubris – the overweening pride – that is Volpone's great vice is, at least, on the grand scale.

We need not waste too much sympathy on Celia. She may be sensible, as well as moral, in refusing Volpone, since the reality of being his mistress could hardly live up to the ecstasies of his imagination; but, despite the miserable circumstances of her marriage, she isn't even tempted. She is virtuous, but she is also a prude who asks for her face to be flayed for 'seducing/ Your blood to this rebellion'. In any case Celia remains too shadowy a figure for us to take her position with too much seriousness.

Volpone leaps upon her, but Bonario, who has come within earshot, melodramatically intervenes in the nick of time and, somewhat sententiously, leads her away to safety, threatening to bring Volpone to justice. Volpone is 'unmasked, unspirited, undone' – temporarily, at least.

Lines 7–151

presently Immediately.
except Except what.
move Urge.
horn-mad Mad at the thought of being cuckolded.
train Trick.
what my engagements are How far I am committed.
means Financial resources. Corvino is using the language of a commercial venture.
And for your fame/That's such a jig There's no need to make such a song and dance about your reputation.
Be jealous still Be quick to resent any slur on your honour.
quirk Twist and turn.
critic Expert.
And If.
honest polity A good stroke of business.
Only of price Uniquely excellent.
rotchet Roach.
aquafortis Nitric acid.
corsives Corrosives.
watched her time Waited for her time to be obstinate.
An errant locust An arrant plague.
Expecting Devising.
cope-man A merchant, or dealer.
mazed Amazed.
left my practice Given up my attempt.

Lines 153–272

the blue Proteus Proteus, the sea-god, changed his shape continually, but Volpone would have changed shape to equal him.
Valois Henry of Valois was entertained in Venice in 1574.
Antinous A beautiful young man, who was admired by the Emperor Hadrian.
prove Try.
serene Blight.
a rope of pearl … Egyptian queen caroused Cleopatra put pearls in Antony's wine.
carbuncle A red gem. Nobody has successfully explained the reference to St Mark's eyes.
Lollia Paulina The wife of the Emperor Caligula; she wore fantastic quantities of jewels.
Though nature lost her kind Even though it would be the last of its kind.

July-flowers Gillyflowers (clove-scented pinks, stocks, wallflowers).
antic Jig.
Ovid's tales The Metamorphoses.
Erycine Venus.
Sophy Shah.
the Grand Signor The Sultan of Turkey.
transfuse Make flow from one into the other.
pined Tormented with envy.
sounds man Proclaims you a man.
disfavour Disfigure.
Nestor's hernia Nestor's impotence.
abuse my nation Destroy my nation's reputation (for lustfulness).
dross Refers to Volpone's gold.

Act 3, Scene 8

Mosca enters, 'bleeding', wounded by Bonario. He and Volpone both wish they were dead. Volpone proposes a suicide pact, though the vigour of his language suggests that he is not yet, in fact, done for. There is a knock at the door. It is Signior Corbaccio. Volpone returns to his couch. Life goes on.

Lines 7–20
engagèd At stake.
like Romans By suicide.
like Grecians Merrily.
the Saffi Bailiffs.
however Whatever happens.

Act 3, Scene 9

Corbaccio enters, followed by Voltore 'unseen'. Voltore overhears Mosca tell Corbaccio (explanatory sentences will become increasingly complicated from now on!) that his son had arrived, heard that his father was about to disinherit him and had left, bent on parricide. This confirms Corbaccio in his determination to disinherit Bonario. Voltore realizes that he is being double-crossed and reveals himself. Mosca is equal, as always, to the crisis. He easily persuades Voltore that Corbaccio has left his money to Volpone and Bonario, enraged, 'will do some violence on his parent'. Voltore can therefore live 'in double hope'. He will inherit not merely Volpone's money but Corbaccio's as well.

Mosca also sees a chance to get Volpone off the hook. He says that Bonario had come to visit Volpone, had found Celia there, had seized her and made her swear, on pain of death, that Volpone had raped her. In this way he gives Volpone a cover story for when Bonario accuses him of attempted rape, and he can rely upon having Voltore, the great lawyer, on his side. Voltore proposes that the whole thing be referred to the Scrutineo, and Mosca is able to say – surely even he must sigh a little with relief at having slipped on the tight-rope and yet narrowly escaped? – that ' 'twas laboured all, sir, for your good'.

Lines 11–55
tendered Tenderly cared for.
foists Excuses, rogueries.
disclaiming in Disowning.
stated Installed.
success Result.
hapless Unfortunate.
Scrutineo The Venetian Senate House.

Revision questions on Act 3

1 What dramatic ironies can you discover in the meeting between Mosca and Bonario (scene 2)?

2 Contrast the scene (4) involving Volpone and Lady Would-Be with the scene (7) that dramatises the encounter between Volpone and Celia.

3 'Volpone's imagination is rich – but diseased.' How does Act 3 (in particular scene 7) support this claim?

Act 4, Scene 1

The audience is afforded a little relief from the dizzy convolutions of the plot. Sir Pol gives Peregrine a lecture on how to behave when abroad. He has as little self-knowledge as his wife and takes himself as seriously. Though he is so obviously the Englishman abroad, he claims that:

> Within the first week of my landing here,
> All took me for a citizen of Venice. (37–8)

He describes certain idiotic 'projects' for money-making: selling red herrings from Rotterdam; or earning the gratitude of the Great Council of Venice by warning them of the danger of allowing anybody but known patriots to possess tinder-boxes, since potential traitors could easily take their tinder-boxes into the *Arsenale* to blow the place up. He has an even more absurd, Heath Robinson scheme for the early detection of the plague, saving delay for quarantine by fumigating ships with onions (which 'naturally attract th' infection') and bellows kept in perpetual motion by water-works. He goes on to explain to Peregrine (for, though he prides himself on being 'politic', he can't keep his mouth shut) that if he were treacherous he has a plan for selling Venice to the Turks. He confides his diary to Peregrine. It reveals only absurdly trivial details of his life – but everything about himself is important to Sir Pol.

Lines 1–64

a plot Referring to the mountebank scene.
mentioned Asked.
height Latitude.
your phrase Your manner of speaking. 'Your' is used impersonally, though Peregrine pretends to take it personally.
I'll slander … sir Ambiguous: either 'I won't wittily misrepresent you again' or 'I won't slander you by attributing wit to you'.
garb Bearing.
So as … in 'em 'So as to keep myself safe from them'.
Machiavel … Bodin Machiavelli had the reputation of subordinating religion to the needs of the state, and Bodin of recommending toleration.
silver fork The fork had not yet come into general use in England.
metal Quality.
Preposterous Back to front, getting things mixed up.
he has him straight Sums him up immediately.
strips Exposes.
I had read Contarene Gasparo Contarini had published a book on Venice which had been translated into English.
discover Disclose.
correspondence Connections.
one o' the States A member of the Dutch assembly.
that's his mark … cheesemonger Peregrine suggests that the mark, or seal, is merely grease from a candle. Sir Pol takes Peregrine's suggestion seriously, and says that his correspondent is a cheesemonger – so presumably the mark is a cheese stain.
cast Planned.
hoy A small Dutch boat.
defalk Allow a deduction. It is hard to see how Sir Pol hopes to make a fortune by such means, which seems to be a recipe for *losing* money.

Lines 66–144

draw the subtle air Breathe the atmosphere of intrigue.

cautions Precautions which he takes in the hope of winning a pension.

Great Council ... Forty ... Ten Sir Pol refers to the ruling hierarchy of Venice.

means Contacts.

put it in their mouths Tell great men what to say.

arsenale Venice's ships and weapons were kept in the huge Arsenal, which was notorious for its frequent fires.

Sealed Licensed.

Soria Syria.

Lazaretto The place where people were kept in quarantine.

'Twill cost me, in onions Onions were supposed to act as a protection against the plague.

strain Stretch.

Which is the easiest matter of a hundred 'Which is the easiest thing in the world'.

note Patent.

A rat had gnawn ... three beans over the threshold The rat's gnawing of his spur-leathers was supposed to bring bad luck, against which Sir Pol protected himself by throwing three beans over the threshold.

tooth-picks Toothpicks were fashionable; Sir Pol presumably bit his through in the passion of his argument.

ragion del stato Reasons of state.

cheapened sprats Presumably by bargaining.

Act 4, Scene 2

Lady Would-be is in search of her husband and his courtesan. Seeing Sir Pol with Peregrine, she immediately concludes that Peregrine is a whore dressed like a man. When Sir Pol withdraws, Peregrine thinks that Sir Pol has been acting as a bawd for his wife.

Lines 1–47

housed i.e. in a brothel.

plays both, with me i.e. plays fast and loose with me.

I do not care to hinder, but to take him 'I do not want to prevent him, but to catch him in the act.'

it Her complexion.

demerit Deserves blame.

as soon At so early an age.

habit Dress – disguised as a man.

humbled Brought low – referring to his spurs.

I reach you not I do not understand you.

polity Cunning.
bear it through Carry it off.
Froward Perverse.
The Courtier Castiglione's book, *The Courtier*.
solecism A grammatical offence: here, an offence against 'our sex'.
land-siren The Sirens lured sailors on to the rocks.

Lines 48–73

Sporus Nero castrated Sporus so that he could marry him. Lady Would-be now seems uncertain of Peregrine's sex.
historic Epoch-making – but perhaps hysterical.
Whitefriars Whitefriars was inside the City of London, but outside its jurisdiction. It was therefore a sanctuary from the law.
forehead Dignity.
fricatrice Prostitute.
liquid Transplant.
carnival She probably means 'carnal'; but 'carnivals' – feasts before Lent – were famous for their licentiousness.
Who here is fled ... conscience Venice was known to be a tolerant place.
disple Discipline.
use this Act like this.
beg shirts Lady Would-be is pulling at his shirt.
queen-apple i.e. her nose is red on that side, like an apple.

Act 4, Scene 3

Lady Would-be learns her mistake from Mosca. She apologizes to Peregrine in terms that make him even more certain that she is offering herself and that Sir Politic Would-be is also 'Sir Politic Bawd', and he determines to get his revenge for the way Sir Pol has 'practised' upon his 'freshmanship'.

Lines 2–23

quest Request.
protest Proclaim.
callet Prostitute.
the creature i.e. Celia.
see Use. The word, followed by 'conceive', is easily open to misunderstanding.
salt-head Experience, salaciousness.

Act 4, Scene 4

Voltore is ensuring that all the witnesses in the forthcoming trial know the lies that they are going to tell. He and Mosca are co-producers of a play and are fussing over whether the actors know their parts. Mosca moves from Corvino to Voltore to Corbaccio, assuring each in turn that he is sole heir to Volpone's fortune.

Lines 1–22
carriage Procedure.
conveyed Circulated.
burden Part.
the truth i.e. that Corvino was, in fact, offering his wife.
formal Detailed and circumstantial.
But Only.
mummia A medicine made from mummies. Corbaccio is a corpse already.
buffalo i.e. he has the horns of a cuckold.
eat it i.e. the crop, the legacy.
Much Not likely!
Mercury The god of eloquence – and of thieves.
French Hercules Also a symbol of eloquence.

Act 4, Scene 5

The Avocatori indicate with their chatterings that they are far from unprejudiced. Voltore embarks on his masterly piece of oratory, in which he persuades the court that Celia is a 'lewd woman' and a 'close adulteress'; that Bonario had planned patricide and had blackened Volpone's name by concocting, with Celia, the story about Volpone's attempted rape. Voltore uses all the forensic arts of pathos, moral indignation and bland assertion. The rhythms of the speech are well oiled and smooth, and he has the answer to every possible objection. If it be said that Celia 'has ever been held/Of unreproved name', then that is because she 'wants no artificial looks, or tears,/To help the visor she has now put on'; and if 'the young man's fame was ever fair, and honest', then 'So much more full of danger is his vice'.

Voltore has his witnesses lined up. Corbaccio has been well programmed and denounces his son as soon as he is switched on. Corvino, with relish, describes his wife as 'a whore/Of most hot exercise' – though, of course, it is precisely because she is *not* a whore that all this trouble has arisen: and he describes in circumstantial detail finding her 'glued' to Bonario, so with almost masochistic glee, publicly proclaiming himself a cuckold. Celia faints, which makes the 4th Avocatore, who seems even more of an idiot than his fellow justices, remark suspiciously, 'This woman has too many moods.'

Mosca gives evidence that Bonario wounded him (which, at least, is true) and Lady Would-be is called to give evidence, at Mosca's instigation, that Celia had been seen, 'with her loose eyes and more lascivious kisses' in a gondola with a strange knight.

Lines 9–87
example Precedent.
after times Future possibilities.
cited Summoned.
frontless Shameless.
close Secret.
timeless Untimely, ill-advised.
owe Own, acknowledge.
extirp extirpate.
heart ...... crimes See how their crimes give them courage.
fact Act.
Preserve himself Remain.
ills Evils.
confederacy Conspiracy.
stale Lure.
collections Conclusions.

Lines 89–146
ends Aims.
sols Sous.
creature Human being.
Abhors his knowledge Abhors to have to acknowledge him.
portent Freak.
made Put you up.
Of most hot exercise Very lustful; 'hot stuff'.
partridge Partridges were reputed to be the most lustful of birds.
Neighs, like a jennet Makes the mating calls of a horse.
well-timbered Well-built.
here On his forehead, where his horns grow.
onward On her way.
laid Calculated.
take Put a spell on, deceive.
baited Enticed.

Act 4, Scene 6

Lady Would-be describes Celia as a 'chameleon' harlot, though Celia is one of the few characters in the play who is *not* a chameleon. Lady Would-be then apologizes profusely for the bad manners of her strong language and has to be soothed by the combined efforts of the Avocatori.

Bonario and Celia are asked what witnesses they can bring. They can answer only 'Our consciences/And Heaven that never fails the innocent'. But as the 4th Avocatore says, with an irony of which he is wholly unaware, 'These are no testimonies'; and Bonario replies, 'Not in your courts,/Where multitude, and clamour, overcomes.'

Voltore now plays his trump card: Volpone is brought in, made up to appear a pathetic picture of impotent decrepitude. Voltore points to him with triumphant sarcasm:

> pray you, mark these hands.
> Are they not fit to stroke a lady's breasts? (27–8)

It is a tribute to Volpone's professionalism that he hasn't, like many amateur actors, forgotten to make up his hands.

Bonario says that he wants Volpone 'proved'. Voltore proposes, in order that the idea may be rejected as absurd, that Volpone be put to the trial with goads, branding-irons, the rack and the strappado. Even Volpone, who is not given to failure of nerve, has to admit later (5, 2, 38) that he sweated a little. Voltore concludes with the barefaced assertion, of which his own performance is the best proof, that 'Damned deeds are done with greatest confidence.' He has proved that white is black by reminding the court that villains can easily prove that black is white.

Celia and Bonario are led away to await sentence. Mosca, who has produced this farce so expertly, assures each legacy-hunter in turn that they are still top of Volpone's list. Volpone and Mosca have achieved a marvellous recovery from a dangerous situation; but it isn't in their nature to leave well alone.

Lines 2–49

chameleon This small lizard is a symbol of deception because of the way it can change its colour to blend with different backgrounds.

hyaena The hyena is also considered a treacherous beast because it attracts its victims with its human cry.

exorbitant Outrageous.

pertinacy Lady Would-be probably means 'impertinence'.

proved Tested.

strappado A torture in which the victim's hands are tied behind his back, he is raised on a pulley, and dropped with a jerk.
thou Refers to Bonario.
equal Just.
fable Falsehood.

Lines 51–92
fleshed Inured, like a dog which has tasted blood.
constancy Resolution.
prodigies Monsters.
want living Lack a livelihood.
the other His prostitution of Celia.
Rest … eyes Rest easy.
Bountiful bones Sarcastic about the mean old scarecrow.
Worthy his age To live to such a miserable old age.
take you no notice i.e. ignore the arrangements I am making with Corbaccio about the will.

Revision questions on Act 4

1 Show how satire and farce are mingled in the first two scenes of Act 4.

2 'The operation of justice in *Volpone* is incompetent or corrupt.' How far would you agree, on the evidence provided by the court scenes of Act 4?

3 What examples of 'acting' can you identify in Act 4?

Act 5, Scene 1

Volpone, safely back in his fox-hole, is enormously relieved at his narrow escape. He needs a few quick drinks to restore him to his normal self.

Lines 1–4
brunt Crisis.
this fled moment The moment that has just past.
Cavè Look out! Perhaps addressed to the audience.
breathe Relax a moment.

Act 5, Scene 2

Mosca appears, full of high spirits and self-congratulation. Volpone says that he enjoyed fooling the court 'more than if I had enjoyed the wench': the thrill of acting and deception for its own sake is the greatest joy of his life; that is why, though Mosca prudently says,

> Here must we rest; this our masterpiece:
> We cannot think, to go beyond this. (13–14)

Volpone cannot resist another stratagem. Castrone and Nano are sent out to proclaim in the streets that Volpone is dead. Volpone makes out a will leaving all his possessions to Mosca, and intends to hide behind a curtain so that he can gloat over the miseries of Voltore, Corbaccio and Corvino when they discover that all their hopes have come to nothing. Mosca is delighted with the scheme – not surprisingly, since Volpone has no suspicion that Mosca might double-cross him; and Volpone is so exhilarated by his success so far that he sees no danger in the plan. He is becoming as blind as his victims. Success has made him 'wanton', as, earlier in the play, it had made Mosca.

Voltore, the vulture with the 'quickest scent' for carrion, is first on the scene. Mosca puts on his master's gown and pretends to be making an inventory of Volpone's goods.

Lines 15–62
prize Masterpiece.
borne it Carried if off.
glebe Soil.
rare Rarely.
sweat Sweated – i.e. you were afraid.
cozened Cheated.
aggravate Put emphasis on.
figures Figures of speech.
shift a shirt Presumably because the vehemence of his oratory made him sweat.
jig Some sport.
with constancy/Sadly Seriously and with a straight face.

Lines 70–111
take upon thee Pretend.
count-book Account book.
parcels Items.
dull Insensible.
clarissimo Grandee. Mosca refers to Corbaccio.
crump ... hog-louse Curl up like a wood-louse.
poetical girdle The girdle of Venus which could transform even the most ugly.

Acrisius The father of Danae. Jove reached Danae in a shower
of gold, although she was strongly guarded.
Makes Gives.
Play the artificer Invent tortures.

Act 5, Scene 3

As well as Voltore, Corbaccio and Corvino soon 'muster',
followed by Lady Would-be. Mosca coolly goes on counting
before handing over the will. The others gather greedily round
to read it. Volpone, concealed, licks his lips over

> How their swift eyes run over the long deed,
> Unto the name, (18–19)

Voltore, who is expert at reading legal documents, is the first
to learn the truth; Corbaccio, who is half blind, deaf and gaga,
is the last. Mosca tortures them by calmly counting his possessions – most of which have come in the form of 'gifts' from
the others – while explaining meekly that 'it is a fortune
thrown upon me ... not my seeking' (lines 31–2). When they
protest they are dismissed one by one with the reminder that
Mosca has so much damaging information about them that
there is nothing they can do. Lady Would-be is told to 'Go
home and use the poor Sir Pol, your knight, well'. Corvino,
the 'wittol', is also sent home, to be 'melancholic, or mad',
which is only too likely, since he has been on the verge of
insanity all through the play. Mosca has to be even more
brutal to Corbaccio, who is so senile that he might not see the
point if for himself:

> Go home, and die, and stink;
> If you but croak a syllable, all comes out: (74–5)

There is no need to spell out the situation to Voltore. Mosca
blandly says that Voltore doesn't need the money since he can
make all that he wants out of the law. With smooth politeness
he turns the knife by saying,

> Good sir, I thank you for my plate: 'twill help
> To set up a young man. Good faith, you look
> As you were costive: best go home and purge, sir. (99–101)

In some of his cadences and attitudes Mosca anticipates
Uriah Heep.

Volpone emerges, overjoyed. Mosca is sent out into the

streets, in Volpone's *clarissimo* clothes, to torment them more, and Volpone wishes that he had some disguise in which he could join in the fun. Mosca undertakes to make a *commendatore* drunk (an easy task apparently!) and bring Volpone the uniform.

Lines 3–51

tissue A rich cloth shot with gold.
Is his thread spun Is he dead?
diaper ... damask Both are types of linen.
suits of hangings Sets of hangings for a four-poster bed.
garters i.e. let them hang themselves in their own garters.
gasp Last gasp.
Old glazen-eyes Corbaccio wears spectacles, and is stumbling through the will on his own.
salt Salt-cellar.
riddles Secrets.
wittol Cuckold.

Lines 58–119

extraordinary In title only. Corvino is not, in fact, a cuckold, but has to allow himself to be thought one.
With the three legs i.e. two legs and a stick.
mar'l Marvel.
travails Labours.
causes Law-suits.
obstreperous Vociferous.
costive Constipated.
commendatori Sergeants at law.
The Fox fares ever best, when he is cursed Proverbial: the fox is cursed only when he escapes.

Act 5, Scene 4

Peregrine enters, 'disguised', to revenge himself on Sir Pol, though he declares that his intention is to 'fright him, only'. He has persuaded some merchants to help him.

The disguised Peregrine warns Sir Pol that the real Peregrine was a spy who had reported to the authorities his plot to sell the state to the Turk and that he is about to be arrested. Sir Pol, in despair, hides in a tortoise-shell, a curious device which he has prepared for just such an emergency. (The tortoise seems to have been a symbol of 'policy': it was also an emblem of silence and prudence – the qualities of which Sir Pol has so blatantly proved incapable.) The Merchants come in, prod and kick the tortoise a little, and Sir Pol is pulled out of his shell. Sir Pol is left to be the laughing-stock of the newspapers and, worse, the pubs.

The scene is fairly crude broad farce, but it is not an inappropriate ending for Sir Pol.

Lines 4–84
Zant A Venetian possession in Greece.
his gulled story The story of his deception.
Know your approaches Get ready to enter.
him whole His whole time.
possess him Have his company.
punk Prostitute.
All the better i.e. all the better for the prosecution. Plays were often thought of as being treasonable.
a frail were rare A round fruit-basket would be the very thing.
engine Device.
Fitted Suited.
device Invention.
motion A puppet-play.
the term The law term.
The freight of the *gazetti* 'In the papers'.
ordinaries Taverns.

Act 5, Scene 5

Mosca is disguised as a *Clarissimo*, Volpone as a *Commendatore*. When Volpone goes out Mosca gives the first direct indication that he intends to outmanoeuvre Volpone: when the fox is out of his hole he is vulnerable, and Mosca is laying his 'fox-trap'.

Lines 4–9
hold/My made one Keep up my assumed role.
borrowed case Disguise.
composition Agreement.

Act 5, Scene 6

Corbaccio and Corvino are planning to go back to the court, to tell as much of the truth as they dare. They can hardly hope to get anything out of this, but at least they may hope to bring Mosca down with them.

Volpone enters and, in terms of mock innocence, congratulates them on their newly inherited 'wealth'. When they curse him, he praises Corvino for not being 'over-leavened, with your fortune'. Some people, he implies, would have let it go to their heads. Like Mosca, he is skilled in mental torture, turning the screw with artistic delicacy.

Lines 5–25
come upon him Demand it from Mosca.
errant Arrant.
You mock ... change wills 'You are mocking everybody, for did not he make you his heir as you had made him your heir?'
over-leavened Puffed up, like bread which has too much yeast.
ha' some ... wine-fat 'Some people would swell up like a winevat.'
very True, i.e. in her unfaithfulness.
bear it out Carry it off.
You will not be aknown You do not want to known (to be the heir).

Act 5, Scene 7

Voltore enters, fuming. Volpone, in tones of sycophantic footlicking, asks for first refusal of a brothel which, he says, Voltore has just acquired with the rest of his goods.

Lines 2–20
make legs Bow.
fingering The allusion is to the skilful playing of an instrument.
reparations Repairs.
Piscaria Fish market.
customed Well patronised.
(none dispraised) With no offence to the others.
refusal First refusal.
candle-rents Rent from property which is deteriorating.
decrease Presumably a deliberate malapropism for 'increase'.

Act 5, Scene 8

Volpone now pretends to Corvino and Corbaccio that he has heard the news of their misfortune and expresses innocent surprise that the worldly-wise Corvino should have been so easily persuaded, like the crow in the fable, to drop his cheese. Corvino threatens violence and Volpone escapes.

Lines 1–27
our habit The habit of Clarissimo.
brooked Liked.

bane Ruin.
traded Experienced.
moral emblems An emblem was an engraving with a poem
  attached to it. Volpone is thinking of the crow who dropped his
  cheese in order to sing to the fox.
jolt-head Blockhead.
chequeens Corvino is referring to the gilt buttons on the
  'sergeant's' gown.
basilisk A fabulous reptile which could kill with a look.

Act 5, Scene 9

Volpone enjoys himself at Voltore's expense by suggesting
that Voltore is only pretending not to have inherited the
money, in order to 'blind the rest'.

Lines 1–12
flesh-fly Blow-fly, which is what the name 'Mosca' means.
biggin A lawyer's cap.
familiar Someone of the same household.
I am mad I am furious that.
Justinian The Roman Emperor who codified Roman law.
ride an advocate Lawyers rode mules, but here the 'mule' is
  riding the lawyer.
quirk Trick.
gullage Being tricked.

Act 5, Scene 10

A scene of utter, deliberate confusion. Voltore, in a state of
probably genuine distraction, appears to want to confess at
least part of the truth to the court – not, of course, out of any
love of truth for its own sake, but out of a vengeful desire to
incriminate Mosca. He says that Mosca has been 'the instrument of all'. Volpone, still in his disguise as *commendatore*, is
sent out to fetch Mosca. Corvino fears that Voltore will say
too much and thinks that 'nought now/Can help, but im-
pudence' (lines 14–15). Corbaccio has little idea of what is
going on, since he is too deaf to hear and moves in a dimension
of his own. Corvino reveals that Volpone is dead, which seems
to prove that at the earlier trial 'he was no deceiver', and that
Mosca has inherited the money. This last piece of information
makes the Avocatori regret that they have not sent for Mosca
via a more 'public officer', since Mosca, being wealthy, is now

respectable and important; so the Notary is sent with a more polite message. Corvino and Corbaccio (in so far as he is conscious) are determined to stick to their original story, but Voltore has handed notes to the bench showing that the original story is a fraud. The Avocatori are, not surprisingly, in a state of brain-splitting confusion.

Lines 4–49

win upon Overcome.

passion Anger, madness.

made/The thing, he gaped for Has achieved the thing Voltore wanted.

but he may be some-deal faulty Mosca, too, was at fault.

modesty Moderation.

confer Examine, compare.

public officer Volpone, in his disguise as a *commendatore*.

you The Notary.

The false spirit The spirit by which, Corvino says, Voltore is possessed.

Act 5, Scene 11

Volpone curses himself for bringing this situation upon himself 'out of mere wantonness'. He learns from Nano that Mosca has taken the keys of his house and now begins to suspect what Mosca is up to. He again cures himself:

> What a vile wretch was I, that could not bear
> My fortune soberly? (15–16)

But he consoles himself that Mosca may still be truer than he fears; and that he may still be able to dissuade Voltore from revealing the truth, by dangling 'new hopes' before him.

Lines 6–21

gave it second Seconded it.

sear up Cauterize; a method of stopping the flow of blood with a hot iron.

kitlings Kittens.

conceits Schemes.

I must be merry, with a mischief to me 'I had to be merry, and see the bad luck it has brought me!'

crotchets Whims.

conundrums Tricks.

His meaning ... my fear 'He may intend better than I fear he does.'

Unscrew my advocate, upon new hopes 'Change my advocate from his present course by dangling new hopes before him'.

Act 5, Scene 12

The Avocatori are desperately trying to puzzle out, from Voltore's notes, what his new story is. Corvino is still trying to persuade the court that Voltore is 'possessed'. Volpone returns and manages to whisper to Voltore that

> the parasite
> Willed me to tell you, that his master lives; (15–16)

so Voltore can still hope to inherit the goods. On Volpone's suggestion, Voltore falls down as though he were indeed possessed, and Volpone gives a vivid description of the symptoms. (He has not lost his capacity for hyperbolic language.) When he 'comes to', Voltore denies that the writing on the 'notes' is his. He then tells the Avocatori that Volpone is alive and denies that he ever said that he was dead.

Mosca enters, so finely dressed and obviously wealthy that the 4th Avocatore immediately thinks him,

> were Volpone dead
> A fit match for my daughter. (50–1)

Volpone appeals to him to support his story that he is alive. Mosca refuses, and tells the court that Volpone is dead. The 1st and 2nd Avocatori are amazed at this twist in affairs, but the 4th Avocatore can only see a prospective son-in-law. Mosca asks Volpone to give him half his goods. Volpone refuses, then changes his mind, but by then Mosca has raised his price. Voltore and Volpone both try to maintain that Volpone is still alive, so Mosca, now a very important person, goes into a pretended sulk. Volpone, a mere *commendatore*, is seized and ordered to be whipped. Realizing that he has nothing to lose, Volpone 'puts off his disguise': if he is to go down he is determined that Mosca shall go down with him.

Corvino tries desperately to intervene to save himself. The 2nd Avocatore says that 'Nothing can be more clear,' which must surely be an overstatement. Bonario puts in a pious truism to the effect that 'Heaven could not, long, let such gross crimes be hid' (line 98), though the revelation of the truth owes more to the fact that thieves, notoriously, cannot be true to one another. Celia, virtuous to the last, puts in a little plea for mercy for the villains.

The villains are called forth for sentence. It is difficult to see how the Avocatori can have understood all that has happened but, mercifully, Jonson has no desire to explain it all again. Mosca is sentenced first. Not the least of his crimes appears, in the eyes of the court, to be the fact that he has dressed out of his class. He is to be whipped and to spend the rest of his life in the galleys. All Volpone's goods are confiscated and given to the hospital of the *Incurabili*, which is particularly appropriate since Volpone has asserted the marvellous medicinal powers of gold. He himself is to be imprisoned until he develops the diseases which he has so long and profitably pretended to have. Voltore, who has banished truth from the courts, is banished from the state. Corbaccio is to be confined in a monastery, where he can learn – it is the only possible thing that is left for him – to die well. Comically, even pathetically, he does not hear the sentence that is passed on him. Corvino is to be rowed through the Grand Canal 'wearing a cap, with fair, long, ass's ears', and then he is to be pilloried. In a curious sense he will thus achieve his unconscious wish to make a public laughing-stock of himself. Celia is returned to her father with three times her dowry; Bonario inherits his father's estate.

So the play comes to a sternly moral ending. Justice, moral and poetic, is done. Jonson could hardly have ended his play in any other way, considering the crimes of which his characters have been guilty. But Jonson has it both ways: he makes Volpone appear again to face his other judges: the audience. Volpone reminds them that it was only a play and that he has, after all, done his audience no harm. As chief entertainer, he appeals for applause.

Lines 12–90

varlet The word is not derogatory; a sergeant was known as a 'varlet'.

how you stood affected How you would behave.

Stop your wind Hold your breath.

vomits crooked pins This, and subsequent details, are imitated from accounts of people who were bewitched – or pretended to be.

all this i.e. Voltore's notes.

proper Handsome.

o' the hinge Going well.

busy Officious.
quick While still alive.
come about Reversed.
his own knave Voltore.
avarice's fool Corbaccio.

Lines 91–157
chimera Refers to Corvino. A chimera was a monster composed
of lion, goat and serpent.
wittol Cuckold.
let's not now despair it i.e. let's have the sentence as quickly as
possible.
Bane Death.
Incurabili A Venetian hospital founded for the treatment of
incurable venereal disease.
berlino The pillory.
fact Crime.
fare jovially Live happily – but also, like Jove, decide our fate.

Revision questions on Act 5

1 Contrast the relationship between Volpone and Mosca in
Act 5 with that displayed in Act 1.

2 It could be argued that Jonson set out to make the action
of the final Act of *Volpone* deliberately confusing. Why
might he have done this?

3   'To make a snare, for mine own neck! and run
   My head into it, wilfully! with laughter!
   When I had newly scaped, was free and clear!'
How and why does Volpone bring down ruin on himself in
the last Act?

The characters

Jonson names most of his characters after animals or birds. Volpone, of course, is The Fox; 'Mosca' means 'fly' or 'parasite'. Voltore, Corbaccio and Corvino are 'the vulture', 'the raven' and 'the crow'. Sir Politic Would-be's name shortens to Sir Pol: he is 'the parrot', and therefore a chatterer. Peregrine is not only 'a traveller' but also 'a hawk'. Moreover, there are constant references in the text to other beasts – apes, asses, crocodiles, mules, gennets, wolves, hyenas, chameleons, tortoises. The naming of the characters suggests – what the events of the play amply justify – the ease with which human beings may lapse into the bestial.

The producer of the play has to decide to what extent to dress his characters like the beasts after which they are named. There are references in the text to The Fox's red hair, eyebrows and whiskers, and Mosca dresses him in his furs. Voltore's lawyer's gown may easily be made to look like a vulture's wings, and make-up and costuming may be used to suggest the rapaciousness of the other legacy-hunters.

Jonson's characters do not lend themselves to detailed analysis: all their traits are plainly there on the surface. It has been said they are two-dimensional, that they are caricatures (though it is worth remembering that caricature is itself an art), and this is true; but they are intensely alive creations who obey the simple laws of their own being. They are totally themselves, revealed in the vitality of the language in which they express their thoughts and emotions, their hopes and schemes. They cannot be taken out of the play in which they appear; they exist only as aspects of the great imaginative act which is *Volpone*.

Volpone

Volpone, himself, is one of Jonson's greatest creations. He is energetic, self-delighting, larger-than-life, virile. Mosca tells Corvina that 'the Turk is not more sensual in his pleasures' than he, and his only children are

> Bastards,
> Some dozen, or more, that he begot on beggars,
> Gipsies, and Jews, and black-moors, when he was drunk.
>
> (1, 5, 45)

The moralists – and we are all moralists at times – can enjoy themselves at his expense, pointing out how he over-reaches himself and how richly he deserves his come-uppance at the end.

The same can be said of a somewhat similar, but even larger, character, Falstaff, who is rejected at the end of *Henry IV, Part 2*. But there is a difference. Falstaff belongs to a much larger world which he really does menace. For better or worse, there can be no place for him at Henry V's court, still less at the Battle of Agincourt. His rejection is vital to the whole dramatic scheme. By comparison the world of *Volpone* is hermetically sealed. It is legitimate and interesting to speculate what Falstaff would have done and said if he had survived to the time of the Battle of Agincourt; but it is neither legitimate nor interesting to speculate what would have happened if Volpone had successfully raped Celia. This is not merely because Celia is little more that a beautiful cipher and is always safe. The point is that what we are really watching, simultaneously enjoying and criticising, is Volpone's exuberant lust. We are marvelling that the force of his lust for Celia should be able to overcome even the equally vigorously expressed force of his greed. At the end he gets what the moralists would call his 'just deserts'; but our satisfaction in this is primarily artistic rather than moral.

Mosca

The play's other main character is Mosca (the fly) – light, quick, infinitely flexible, buzzing and stinging. He is clever, scheming and treacherous: having made fools of all the other characters who hoped to inherit from the supposedly dead Volpone, he then attempts to betray his master, whose goods he covets. In court, he pretends that Volpone is really dead and that he does not know the man who claims to be his master. In asides to Volpone, Mosca tries to extort much of Volpones wealth, as the price of admitting the truth (5, 12, 55ff). Mosca is indeed the character 'we love to hate'. But at least he never deceives himself; he is fully aware of his place in the parasitical chain.

Voltore

Voltore (or vulture) is perhaps the least individual of the three principal dupes who are victims both of Volpone and of their own greed. Voltore has no family, or at any rate none is referred to, and we see him only in is 'professional' capacity as a lawyer. He has no wife to prostitute or son to disinherit. Voltore might be said, however, to prostitute his legal knowledge by using all his considerable skill to argue for the wrong side in court (Act 4). He will speak out only for money; truth and justice don't come into it. In this, Mosca indicates (Act 1, scene 3), he is like other lawyers. Jonson uses the character of Voltore to make large satirical swipes at the legal profession, a familiar target then and since. Particular stress is laid on his learning and intelligence, and his folly is therefore intensified – a point rubbed in by Volpone and Mosca in Act 5.

Corvino and Celia

It is no use asking whether, in real life, a human being would behave like *Corvino*: would at one moment be so insanely jealous of his beautiful young wife Celia for leaning out of a window, that he draws a chalk line beyond which he will not allow her to pass: and at the next moment would be forcing her to go to bed with another man. As a matter of fact the answer to such a question is, 'Yes: the evidence of history and psychology is that human beings are indeed capable of such behaviour'; but that is not the point. The point is that Jonson *makes it happen.* In the moral sphere it is an example of the transforming and dehumanizing power of gold, but the play is not primarily a moral treatise and the characters are not illustrative 'types'; the play is an act of dramatic creation, and so are the characters.

The virtuous *Celia* seems to have strayed in from another world. As we have said before, she is little more than a beautiful cypher, reacting throughout with a consistent moral rectitude: first, to her husband's unreasoning jealousy; then –

as cupidity overthrows his scruples – to his complete *volte face*; and, lastly, to Volpone's terrifying lust for her.

Sir Politic and Lady Would-be

Sir Politic Would-be is a perfect example of the 'silly ass' to be found in so many later English comedies. He is pompous, conceited and ineffably foolish; he is easily duped by Volpone and Mosca.

Lady Would-be, on the other hand, is a comic creation of genius. She is a well-known type, and could easily have remained merely a type, but Jonson invests her with overwhelming vitality so that the scene in which she visits Volpone is a comic *tour-de-force*. Volpone's own superabundant ego and brio are reduced to quivering jelly by the 'eternal tongue' of this monstrous woman who has the brazen vulgarity to address him as 'Volp'. Having reduced Volpone by her chatter to a miserable cringing parody of himself, she says,

> Come, in faith, I must
> Visit you more a days; and make you well:
> Laugh, and be lusty. (3, 4, 112–15)

She is wholly unconscious that she is the only person who can *prevent* Volpone from laughing and being lusty, and that she is the sole cause of his illness. Moreover, it is her presence that is keeping him from Celia.

Corbaccio and Bonario

Corbaccio is described in 'The Persons of the Play' as 'an old gentleman' and his part in the play is the caricature of such a person. He is a deaf old dodderer, yet foolishly imagines he will outlive Volpone; he thus becomes another of the legacy hunters and another easy dupe for Volpone and Mosca. Mosca persuades him to disinherit his son Bonario and leave all his money to Volpone, thus convincing Volpone of his disinterested love and friendship.

Bonario is, with Celia, practically the only straight, honest character in the play – as a result there is not very much one can say about him. However, it is he who, posted by Mosca to overhear his father promising Volpone that he will disinherit his son, overhears instead Volpone's attempt to seduce Celia.

He rushes into Volpone's room and rescues Celia – which doesn't prevent Volpone from later insinuating to Corvino that he has been successful with Celia:

> Troth, your wife has shown
> Herself a very woman: but, you are well,
> You need not care, (5, 7, 20–22)

Themes and style

Themes

Greed and lust are the principal themes of the play. The predatory birds wait to feed on the corpse of the fox (Volpone). When they hear that the fox is dead, they 'muster' instantly, snuffing the carrion from afar. The fox uses his cunning, by flattering their hopes, to make the birds drop their cheese. And all the time the parasite adapts himself to whatever body he is living off. Even the 4th Avocatore, at the end, sees a chance of marrying his daughter into money. The play is a tightly knit complex of parasitical inter-relationships.

One thing that can overthrow greed, at least temporarily, is *lust* – which is, after all, only greed in another guise. In Corvino's case, it is a measure of his avarice that it can conquer even his pathological sexual possessiveness, but it is a measure of Volpone's lust that it makes him glad even at the prospect of giving all his wealth to Celia.

Folly and gullibility are exemplified by the greedy characters above. Sir Politic is a different case. The scenes in which he appears are on a different level of comedy from the rest; they are slighter, less intense, and though they relate to the general themes of folly and gullibility they have little to do with the particular theme of greed. Still, they are wittily done, filled out with excellent comic invention, and they fulfil the structural function of providing a rest, a change of key, from the enormities of the legacy hunters.

Parasitism is a central theme of the play. Mosca is the principal parasite, but many of the other characters – certainly all the legacy hunters – can be so described. As the well-known lines have it:

> Big fleas have little fleas
> Upon their backs to bite 'em,
> And little fleas have lesser fleas,
> And so ad infinitum.

Deception and self-deception. These themes, too, are omnipresent. Volpone feigns illness, impersonates the mountebank

Scoto, disguises himself as a *commendatore*. Mosca is the producer, make-up artist, prompter and actor in innumerable
little dramas. Moreover, the dramas are largely extemporized
to meet changing situations. Much of the excitement of the
play is generated by this quick-change artistry. At the moral
level it can be said that many of the characters are not only
deceivers, they are also self-deceivers. (Mosca is an exception;
he knows himself for the parasite he is.) Volpone is blinded by
the very gusto of his pride and success into going too far;
Corbaccio persuades himself that by selling his son he is doing
him a favour; Corvino persuades himself that attempting to
prostitute his wife is an act of charity to Volpone.

The thrill of the chase, and the will to power are over-riding in
Volpone. Even the frustration of his failure to seduce Celia is
banished by the excitement of escaping the hunt. The daemon
which drives him to put himself in increasingly dangerous
situations so that he can escape and laugh at his pursuers
eventually brings his downfall, and it is the same daemon
which gives the plot its humming impetus.

Irony. Above all, Jonson loved irony: it pervades the play –
in its plot, characterization and dialogue. Jokes and ironies
are hidden in every nook and cranny. For example, when
Mosca, faced with the apparently impossible task of bringing
Celia to Volpone's bed, visits Volpone's house, Corvino hopes
and imagines that he has brought the news that Volpone is
dead; but Mosca says that Volpone has recovered through the
use of Scoto's oil, brought to him by Corbaccio and Voltore.
Corvino has just beaten the mountebank away from his
window, yet here, at a single stroke, his triumph is turned to
defeat. Then there is the touch whereby, when Volpone's
goods are confiscated, they are given to the hospital of the
Incurabili. This is particularly appropriate because the hospital
was founded for the clearly unsuccessful treatment of venereal
disease, and Volpone is known to own at least one popular
brothel (5, 8, 12).

Then, again, Mosca reminds us that gold was held to be the
supreme medicine:

> This is true physic, this your sacred medicine,
> No talk of opiates to the great elixir.

It is a beautiful irony that the wonderful gold that Volpone has been at such pains to assemble should be used in the end to alleviate the lot of the incurable.

Style

Neither Jonson's verse nor his characterization have the light and shade or the complexity of Shakespeare's. He sees everything in hard, clear colours. One can argue for hours over the character of Hamlet, or, for that matter, of Shylock, and allow single lines to echo through one's mind. By comparison, Jonson is a poet of the brilliant surface of things, but the world he creates in *Volpone* has the virtues of great concentration and intensity.

And it is Jonson's poetic gift that is able to cram his play with such vitality. His verse is graphic, compressed, racy, idiomatic. Take Mosca's ironic admiration of lawyers:

> Men of your large profession, that could speak
> To every cause, and things mere contraries,
> Till they were hoarse again, yet all be law;
> That, with most quick agility, could turn,
> And re-turn, make knots and undo them;
> Give forked counsel; take provoking gold
> On either hand, and put it up (1, 3, 53–9).

Such verse is notable for its packed muscular power; there is no fat on it; it is colloquial, yet precise and particular, the product of a mind completely in command of its material. Elsewhere, when he wants to, Jonson can screw his verse to an extraordinary pitch of intensity. Here is Corvino's jealousy:

> First, I will have this bawdy light dammed up;
> And, till't be done, some two, or three yards off,
> I'll chalk a line; o'er which, if thou but chance
> To set thy desperate foot ...
> And now I think on't, I will keep thee backwards;
> Thy lodging shall be backwards; thy walks backwards;
> Thy prospect – all be backwards. (2, 6, 50–59)

The restless to-and-fro movement, the way the jealousy rides on its own momentum, the frenetic, jerky, screaming tone are enacted with wonderful economy. This combination of prodigality of detail with economy of expression is a trade-mark of Jonson's work.

General questions and sample answer in note form

1 Many of the characters in *Volpone* are named after beasts. What is the significance of this?

2 'The triumph of "good" at the end of *Volpone* is a formality. Jonson isn't interested in it – nor does he expect his audience to be.' Discuss.

3 'The whole episode of Sir Politic Would-Be never did, nor never can please. He seems to be brought in merely to lengthen out the play.' What is your view?

4 Do you think Jonson differentiates sufficiently between Volpone's 'clients', the dupes who visit his sick-bed? Provide evidence for your point of view.

5 How would you support, or attack, the view that Jonson was a great poet?

6 In what ways do you find the ending of the play satisfactory or unsatisfactory?

7 What is gained by making the action of *Volpone* continuous (i.e. all the events depicted occur within a single day)?

8 In your view does it matter that there is not, arguably, a single sympathetic character in *Volpone*?

9 Comment on the idea of parasitism as a central theme of the play.

10 How would you argue against the view that the characters and events of *Volpone* are so exaggerated that it is impossible to take seriously what Jonson is saying?

11 On the evidence of *Volpone*, comment on Jonson's skill as a constructor of plots.

12 Take a single scene from *Volpone* and explain how you, as director, would stage it to bring out its full dramatic potential. You might discuss key moments of dialogue; lighting effects; costume, make-up, etc.

Suggested notes for essay answer to question 1

More than half a dozen characters, in main plot and sub-plot, are named after animals. This gives to the play the air of a zoo – or, more accurately, a jungle, since the only law that seems to apply is the law of the jungle: the fittest (i.e., strongest and most cunning) will survive by preying on the weaker. The world of *Volpone* is bleak. Jonson shows the distorting effects of greed and folly; his characters are propelled by a single motive force (though Volpone himself is allowed both love/lust and greed). Their human complexity is reduced or denied. Men, and at least one woman (Lady Would-Be), are turned into animals governed by a single appetite. At one level *Volpone* operates as a moral fable, using 'animals' to point a moral. But it is first and foremost a superbly effective drama, not a sermon. Jonson uses 'animal' attributes: external colouring or plumage (see the fuss Lady Would-Be makes over her hair at the start of Act 3, scene 4); the security of camouflage (Volpone playing the invalid or the mountebank); cunning, stealth, quick wits; a literal rapidity of motion (most of the characters spend most of their time scurrying from place to place, trying to make their fortunes or to save themselves from disaster). These attributes, which we may associate with particular beasts (fox, fly, bird of prey), make for a tense, darting drama. Jonson takes a lop-sided, one-dimensional view of human nature, but his vigour and inventiveness override objections.

Further reading

Ben Jonson: Studies in the Plays, C. G. Thayer (University of Oklahoma Press)

The Jacobean Drama, Una Ellis-Fermor (Methuen)

Rhetoric as a Dramatic Language in Ben Jonson, A. E. Sackton (Cassell)